# Where do Babies come from?

**Susan Meredith**

**Designed by Lindy Dark**
**Illustrated by Sue Stitt and Kuo Kang Chen**

**Revised by Philippa Wingate**
**Cover design by Russell Punter**
**Cover illustration by Christyan Fox**
With thanks to Katarina Dragoslavić and Rosie Dickins

Consultants: Dr. Kevan Thorley and
Cynthia Beverton of Relate, Marriage Guidance Council

## CONTENTS

# All about babies

As the baby grows, its mother's tummy gets bigger.

Everybody who has ever lived was once a baby and grew in their mother's tummy. This book tells the story of how babies come into the world and begin to grow up.

A baby grows in a sort of hollow bag called the womb or uterus. This is a warm, safe place for it to be until it is big and strong enough to survive in the outside world.

## Food and oxygen

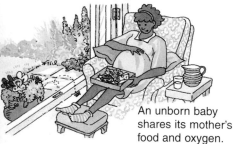

An unborn baby shares its mother's food and oxygen.

The baby needs food to stay alive and grow. It also needs oxygen from the air. But the baby cannot eat or breathe in the womb. It gets food and oxygen from its mother's blood.

## Being born

The baby stays inside its mother for about nine months. That is about 38 weeks. Then it is ready to be born. It gets out of its mother's tummy through an opening between her legs.

## Feeding

At first the only food a baby needs is milk, either from her mother's breasts or from feeding bottles. She needs to be fed every few hours.

## Crying

It is not always easy to work out what a baby's crying means.

A newborn baby can do nothing for herself, so she takes a lot of looking after. Crying is her only way of telling people she needs something.

## Baby animals

Kittens feed on milk from their mother's nipples.

A cow's tummy gets fatter as her calf grows inside her.

Many animals grow in their mothers' tummies and are born in the same way as people. They also get milk from their mothers.

## Growing up

Babies gradually learn to do more and more for themselves.

Many animals separate from their parents when they are very young. It is years before children can manage without their parents' help.

# Starting to grow

Everybody is made of millions of tiny living bits called cells. A baby starts to grow from just two very special cells, one from its mother and one from its father. Together, these two cells make one new cell.

## Dividing cells

Each cell is no bigger than one of the full stops on this page.

The new cell divides in half to make two cells exactly the same. These two cells then divide to make four cells. The cells carry on dividing until a whole ball of cells is made.

## In the womb

Ball of cells

Womb lining

Womb

The ball of cells settles down in the mother's womb, the place where babies grow. It sinks into the womb's soft cushiony lining and carries on growing.

A month later, the developing baby is still no bigger than a baked bean, but the dividing cells have started growing into the different parts of the baby's body.

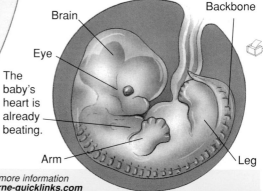

Brain

Eye

The baby's heart is already beating.

Backbone

Arm

Leg

**Internet link** For a link to a website with more information about babies and cells, go to **www.usborne-quicklinks.com**

## The baby's lifeline

The baby is attached to the lining of the womb by a special cord. The food and oxygen the baby needs go from its mother's blood down the cord and into the baby's body.

Like everybody else the baby needs to get rid of waste. This goes down the cord from the baby's blood into its mother's blood. Her body gets rid of it when she goes to the toilet.

Blood vessels

This is called the placenta. It grows on the lining of the womb.

The cord is called the umbilical cord.

The placenta is where food and oxygen, and waste, pass between the mother's blood and the baby's.

The baby floats in a bag of special water. This cushions it from knocks.

The baby can't drown in the water because it doesn't need to breathe until it is born.

## Getting bigger

The baby continues to grow. It moves and kicks, and also sleeps. It can hear its mother's heart beating and noises from outside her body too. Some babies even get hiccups.

Eventually, most babies settle into an upside-down position in the womb.

Some babies suck their thumbs.

# What is it like being pregnant?

When a mother has a baby growing inside her, it is called being pregnant. While she is pregnant, her body changes in all sorts of ways.

## Check-ups
The mother has regular check-ups to make sure she and the baby are healthy. These are given by a midwife or doctor. A midwife is somone who looks after pregnant mothers.

The mother is weighed. She should put on weight as the baby grows.

The mother's blood and urine (wee) are tested. This helps the midwife tell if the mother and baby are well.

## Looking after herself
The mother has to take special care of herself. If she is well, the baby is more likely to be healthy too.

It's not good for the baby if the mother smokes, drinks alcohol or takes certain medicines.

She is feeding her baby as well as herself, so she has to eat healthy food.

The mother's body has to work harder than usual, giving the baby what it needs. She has to rest more.

Gentle exercise pumps more blood through to the baby and makes the mother feel better too.

When the mother's tummy gets big, she should not carry heavy things. She may strain her back.

The midwife feels the mother's tummy. This gives her an idea of the baby's size and position.

She listens to the baby's heart through a special stethoscope. She puts it on the mother's tummy.

## Photos of the baby

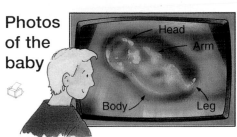

Head
Arm
Body
Leg

A machine called an ultrasound scanner takes moving pictures of the baby in the womb. These appear on a television screen and show everyone how the baby is developing.

## Kicking

After about five months, the mother feels the baby moving. Later, it will kick.

You may feel the kicks if you put your hand on the mother's tummy.

Eventually the mother can see her tummy moving and even guess whether a bump is a hand or a foot.

## Getting bigger

Intestines (food tube)

The skin stretches.

Backbone

Womb

Bladder, where urine is stored

The mother's womb is normally the size of a small pear. As the baby grows, the womb stretches and other things in her body get squashed up. This can be a bit uncomfortable but everything goes back to normal later.

7

# Mothers and fathers

The special cells from the mother and father which make a baby start to grow are the sex cells. They are different from each other.

## Egg cells

The mother's sex cell is called an egg cell or ovum. She has lots of egg cells stored in her body, near her womb.

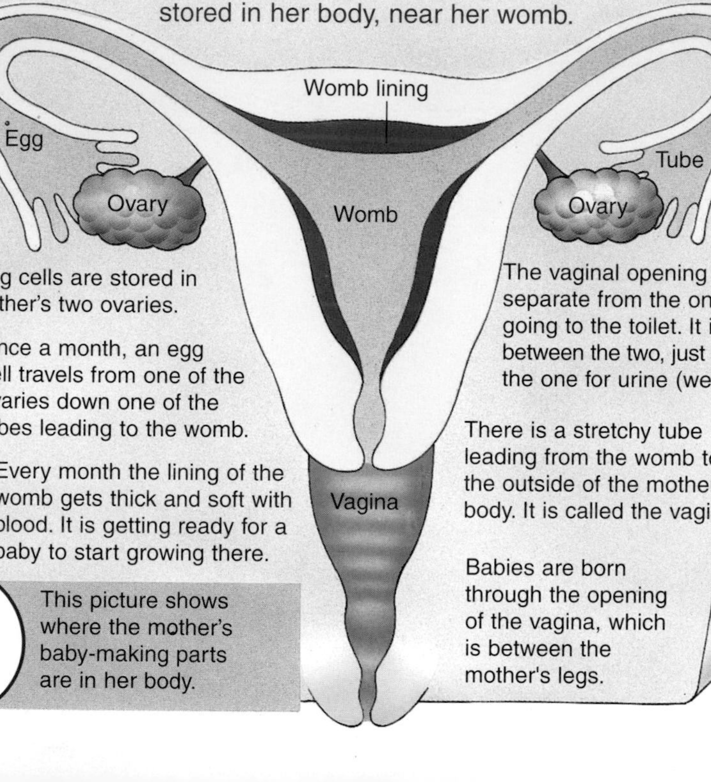

Womb lining

Egg

Tube

Ovary

Womb

Ovary

Vagina

The egg cells are stored in the mother's two ovaries.

Once a month, an egg cell travels from one of the ovaries down one of the tubes leading to the womb.

Every month the lining of the womb gets thick and soft with blood. It is getting ready for a baby to start growing there.

The vaginal opening is quite separate from the ones for going to the toilet. It is between the two, just behind the one for urine (wee).

There is a stretchy tube leading from the womb to the outside of the mother's body. It is called the vagina.

Babies are born through the opening of the vagina, which is between the mother's legs.

This picture shows where the mother's baby-making parts are in her body.

## Sperm

The father's sex cell is called a sperm cell. Sperm are made in the father's two testicles. The testicles are in the bag of skin which hangs behind his penis (willy).

Tube

Penis

Testicle

The father's baby-making parts are between his legs.

Sperm can travel from the testicles along two tubes and out of the end of the penis.

Urine never comes out of the penis at the same time as sperm.

## Growing up

Young girls and boys cannot become mothers and fathers. Your baby-making parts don't start working until your body starts to look like a grown-up's.

## What if a baby doesn't start?

If a baby does not start to grow, the womb's thick lining is not needed. The lining and the egg cell break up and trickle out of the mother's vagina with some blood.

This takes a few days each month and is called having a period. To soak up what comes out, the mother puts things called tampons in her vagina or pads in her pants.

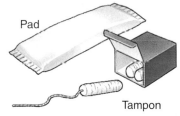

Pad

Tampon

9

# How does a baby start?

A baby starts to grow when an egg and sperm meet and join together. They do this inside the mother's body. The way the sperm get to the egg is through the mother's vagina.

The mother and father cuddle each other very close. The father's penis gets stiffer and fits comfortably inside the mother's vagina. This is called making love or having sex.

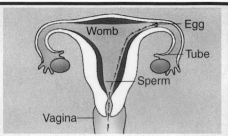

Sperm cells come out of the opening at the end of the penis and swim up into the mother's womb and tubes. If the sperm meet an egg in the tubes, one of them may join with it.

Sperm have long tails which they flick. This helps them to swim.

The moment when the egg and sperm join together is called conception or fertilization. Now a baby can start to grow.

10

## Pregnant or not?

It is several months before the mother's tummy starts to get bigger but she has other ways of knowing she is pregnant.

Calendar

If she is pregnant, her monthly periods stop. The lining of the womb is needed for the growing baby.

Some pregnant mothers feel sick. This is caused by chemicals called hormones in their blood.

The hormones may make the mother go off foods she usually likes; or they may make her crave some foods.

Her breasts get bigger and may feel a bit sore. They are getting ready to make milk when the baby is born.

To be sure she is pregnant, the mother's urine is tested to see if it has one of the pregnancy hormones in it.

11

# How is a baby born?

After nine months inside its mother, the baby is ready to be born. It has to leave the warm, safe womb and move down the vagina to the outside world. This is called labour, which means hard work.

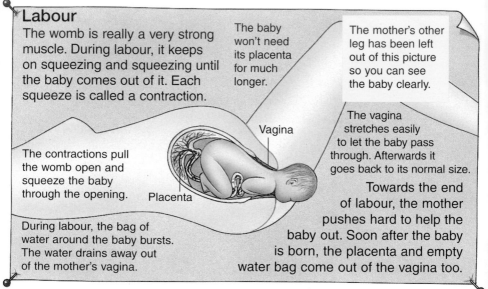

## Labour

The womb is really a very strong muscle. During labour, it keeps on squeezing and squeezing until the baby comes out of it. Each squeeze is called a contraction.

The baby won't need its placenta for much longer.

The mother's other leg has been left out of this picture so you can see the baby clearly.

The contractions pull the womb open and squeeze the baby through the opening.

Vagina

Placenta

The vagina stretches easily to let the baby pass through. Afterwards it goes back to its normal size.

During labour, the bag of water around the baby bursts. The water drains away out of the mother's vagina.

Towards the end of labour, the mother pushes hard to help the baby out. Soon after the baby is born, the placenta and empty water bag come out of the vagina too.

## When does labour start?

When the baby is ready to be born, special hormones are made in its blood. These go down the umbilical cord to the mother's body and make the contractions start.

The mother feels the contractions as pains in her tummy. Most mothers go to hospital to have their baby. Some choose to have theirs at home.

## Helping the mother

Having a baby is exciting but can be exhausting and take many hours. A midwife looks after the mother during labour. The father can help too.

The father might rub the mother's back if it aches, or encourage her to relax and breathe properly.

The mother can have an injection to relieve the pain. Breathing in a mixture of a special gas and air through a face-mask also helps.

## The baby's heartbeat

The midwife listens to the baby's heartbeat during labour to make sure it is all right. In hospitals, the heartbeat is sometimes measured by a machine called a monitor.

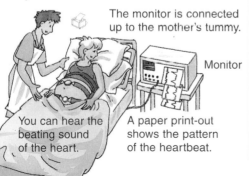

The monitor is connected up to the mother's tummy.

Monitor

You can hear the beating sound of the heart.

A paper print-out shows the pattern of the heartbeat.

## What is a Caesarian birth?

Sometimes the baby can't be born in the usual way. Instead it is lifted out through a cut in the mother's tummy. This is called a Caesarian.

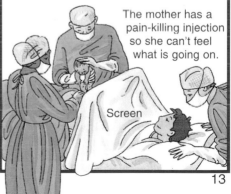

The mother has a pain-killing injection so she can't feel what is going on.

Screen

13

# Newborn babies

The first thing everyone does as soon as a baby is born is to look between its legs.
Is it a girl or a boy?

The midwife checks that there is no liquid in the baby's nose or mouth. Now he can start to breathe.

The cord is cut here. The baby can't feel it.

A clip stops any bleeding.

Now that the baby can breathe and feed for himself, he no longer needs his umbilical cord. It is cut off.

Clip

The tiny bit of cord that is left dries up and falls off in a few days. Your tummy button is where your cord was.

The midwife checks that the baby is well and weighs him. He will be weighed often to make sure he is growing.

In hospital, a newborn baby has a name label put on his wrist. This avoids any mix-up about whose baby he is.

Name label

14

# Getting used to the world

The baby has been safe and comfortable in the womb for nine months. It is probably quite a shock to find herself in the outside world. She may also be tired from the birth.

The baby will get used to her new surroundings better if she is handled and spoken to very gently. It may also help if things are kept quiet and dimly lit at first.

The mother starts feeding the baby.

The parents cuddle the baby and start getting to know her. Sisters and brothers come to meet her.

Newborn babies have to be wrapped up warm. Their bodies lose heat quickly.

Some new babies are almost bald. Others have a lot of hair. Some have hair on their body. This rubs off.

Babies have a soft patch on their head. Bones gradually grow over it, but until then it has to be protected from knocks.

In hospital, babies usually sleep in a cot beside their mother's bed.

## Incubators

If a new baby is very small or unwell, she may have to go in an incubator. This is a see-through cot which is all enclosed and very warm.

The parents can touch the baby through windows in the incubator.

# What makes a baby like it is?

The mother's egg and the father's sperm cell together have all the instructions needed for a baby to grow in the way it does.

## Chromosomes

The instructions are carried on special threads in the cells. The threads are called chromosomes. The proper word for the instructions is genes.

This shows part of a chromosome.

The instructions are in a complicated code a bit like a computer program.

When the egg and sperm join together at conception, the new cell gets the chromosomes from both of them. Copies of these are passed to every cell in the baby's body.

A baby's cells have 46 chromosomes – 23 from the egg and 23 from the sperm.

Because you have chromosomes from both your parents, you will take after both of them. The mixture of the two sets of instructions also means that you are unique.

Some things about you, like the way you look, depend a lot on your chromosomes. Other things depend as well on the type of life you have after you are born.

You are more likely to become a good swimmer if you are taken to the swimming pool a lot.

## Girl or boy?

Whether a baby is to be a girl or a boy is settled at conception. It depends on one chromosome in the egg and one in the sperm. These are the sex chromosomes.

The sex chromosome in all egg cells is called X. Half the sperm also have an X sex chromosome but half have one called Y.

X or Y

If a sperm with an X chromosome joins with the egg, the baby is a girl.

Girls have two X sex chromosomes.

XX

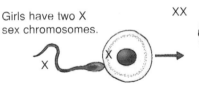

X

If a sperm with a Y chromosome joins with the egg, the baby is a boy.

Boys have one X and one Y sex chromosome.

XY

Y

## Twins

Twins grow in their mother's womb together and are born at the same time, one by one. A few twins are identical, which means exactly alike. Most twins are non-identical, which means not exactly alike.

Sometimes, when the new cell made at conception splits in two, each half grows into a separate baby. These twins are identical because they come from the same egg and sperm.

Identical twins are always the same sex.

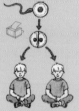

Sometimes, two separate sperm meet and join with two different eggs at the same time, and two babies grow. These twins are not identical because they came from different eggs and sperm.

Non-identical twins may be the same sex or one of each sex.

*Internet link* For a link to a website where you can discover what genes and chromosomes are made of and how they work in our bodies, go to **www.usborne-quicklinks.com**

17

# What do babies need?

Babies need to have everything done for them. They have to be fed and kept warm, comfortable and clean.

They need lots of love and attention, and they need interesting things going on around them.

## Breast-feeding

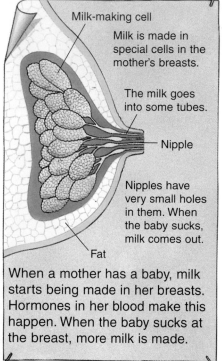

Milk-making cell

Milk is made in special cells in the mother's breasts.

The milk goes into some tubes.

Nipple

Nipples have very small holes in them. When the baby sucks, milk comes out.

Fat

When a mother has a baby, milk starts being made in her breasts. Hormones in her blood make this happen. When the baby sucks at the breast, more milk is made.

If a mother is breast-feeding, she needs to eat well, drink plenty and get extra rest.

Breast milk is made from goodness in the mother's blood and is the best food for a baby. It has chemicals called antibodies in it. These help the baby to fight off illnesses.

## Bottle-feeding

If babies are not being breast-fed, they have special powdered milk instead. This is usually made from cow's milk but is then altered to make it more like breast milk.

Special powdered milk is mixed with water for a baby's bottle.

Ordinary cow's milk is too strong for babies.

## Cuddles

A young baby's neck is not strong enough to hold her head up. Her head needs something to rest on all the time.

A cushion will stop your arm aching.

Babies need a lot of cuddles to make them feel safe and contented. They need to be handled gently though.

Babies cannot fight off germs like older people, so their bottles have to be extra-specially clean. This is done by sterilizing, which means getting rid of germs.

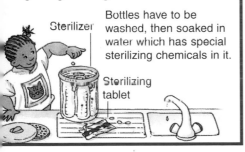

Bottles have to be washed, then soaked in water which has special sterilizing chemicals in it.

Sterilizer

Sterilizing tablet

## Nappies

A young baby may need as many as eight nappy-changes in a day.

If a wet or dirty nappy is not changed the baby is more likely to get an itchy rash.

Babies do not know in advance that they need to go to the toilet. They only learn to tell as they get older.

## Sleeping

Babies have no idea of day and night at first.

It can take them a long time to learn to sleep through the night.

Some young babies sleep for as many as 18 hours a day. They wake up every few hours to feed though, even in the night. Nobody knows why some babies sleep more than others.

19

# A new baby in the family

This is an exciting, enjoyable time but it is also hard work. And it can take a while to get used to having a brand-new person in the family.

A new baby takes up so much of her parents' time and attention that older brothers and sisters can even feel a bit jealous at first.

## The mother's body

It takes a few weeks for the mother's body to go back to normal after having the baby. She needs to rest. Both parents will be tired from getting up in the night to look after the baby.

## Helping

You could fetch things that are needed for the baby and tidy them away.

It is useful for the parents to have help around the house at first. As the baby gets older, you may be able to help by, say, giving her a bottle.

20

## Crying

A baby's crying is hard to ignore. This is useful for the baby: it makes people look after him. Babies cry for various reasons. Nobody really knows why some cry more than others.

Is the baby hungry? Is he uncomfortable or in pain? Is he too hot or too cold, bored, tired, lonely or frightened?

Babies cannot wait for things. They have not learned to think about other people's feelings and if they do have to wait long for something like food, they may even become unwell.

Brothers and sisters can sometimes feel left out.

# Playing with a baby

A new baby will not be able to play with you for some time but she may soon start to enjoy watching you play nearby. Once you start to play with her, try to move and speak gently so you don't startle her. Give her plenty of time to react to things and remember that babies cannot concentrate for long. Never do anything she is not happy about.

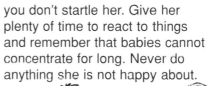

Babies can only see clearly about 25cm (10in) from their nose.

Babies learn about things by putting them in their mouth, so always ask a grown-up if they are safe.

For the first few weeks, a baby probably has enough to do just getting used to her new surroundings. But she will soon start needing lots of things to look at and listen to.

When babies first learn to hold things, they like being given lots of different things to examine. However, they drop them very easily and don't know how to pick them up again.

Once the baby can sit up, he will be able to play with toys more easily.

Once he can crawl, you can give him things that roll.

**Internet link** For a link to a website where you can learn more about newborn babies and what it's like to have a new baby in the family, go to **www.usborne-quicklinks.com**

# Babies in nature

Other babies are made, like people, by a mother and a father. In nature, when parents come together so that their sex cells can meet, it is called mating. The moment when the cells join together is called fertilization.

## Animals

Animals have their babies in a very similar way to people. During mating, sperm swim towards eggs inside the mother's body. If sperm fertilize the eggs, babies grow in the mother's womb. They are born through her vagina and feed on her milk.

Most animals have more than one baby at a time.

Puppies stay in their mother's womb for nine weeks.

## Birds

Baby birds grow outside their mother's body instead of inside. After mating, the mother bird lays her fertilized eggs. Babies grow in the eggs so long as the parents keep them warm by sitting on them.

A growing chick

The chick gets its food from the egg yolk.

Yolk

Air passes through the egg shell so the chick can breathe.

When the chick is ready to be born, it cracks open the egg shell with its beak and hatches out.

Eggs that we eat are unfertilized eggs. Chicks could not have grown in them.

*Internet link* For a link to a website where you can find out the names for over a hundred types of animals and their babies, go to **www.usborne-quicklinks.com**

## Insects

Insects lay eggs after mating and fertilization. Most baby insects do not look much like their parents at first. They go through a big change before they are fully grown.

A caterpillar hatches from a butterfly's egg.

The caterpillar changes into a chrysalis.

The chrysalis becomes a butterfly.

## Fish

Mother fish lay unfertilized eggs. The father then comes along and puts his sperm on them, and babies start to grow.

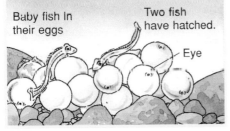

Baby fish in their eggs

Two fish have hatched.

Eye

# Internet links

For links to more websites about babies and birth, go to the Usborne Quicklinks Website at **www.usborne-quicklinks.com** and click on the number of the website you want to visit.

**Website 1** – Follow the development of baby Emma and see how a baby grows from conception to birth.

**Website 2** – Find out what to expect on the first day of a baby's life. This site explains what the new baby will look like, what it will be able to do and what the experience will be like for the new parents.

**Website 3** – Try an online activity and see if you can guess which embryo is human.

**Website 4** – Reproduction facts, animations and quizzes.

# Index

First published in 2001 by Usborne Publishing Ltd., Usborne House, 83-85 Saffron Hill, London EC1N 8RT, England. **www.usborne.com**